mario bellini

:: ARCHITECT AND DESIGNER

 National Gallery of Victoria

NGV INTERNATIONAL 4 DEC 2003 - 22 FEB 2004

MARIO BELLINI

MARIO BELLINI WAS BORN IN 1935 AND GRADUATED IN 1959 AT THE POLITECNICO DI MILANO. HE LIVES AND WORKS IN MILAN. HIS ACTIVITIES RANGE FROM ARCHITECTURE AND URBAN DESIGN TO FURNITURE AND INDUSTRIAL DESIGN.

HIS FAME AS A DESIGNER DATES FROM 1963 WHEN HE BECAME DESIGN CONSULTANT FOR OLIVETTI AND CASSINA. HE HAS SINCE WORKED WITH A VARIETY OF FIRMS IN AND OUTSIDE ITALY, INCLUDING ARTEMIDE, B&B ITALIA, HELLER, NATUZZI, RENAULT, ROSENTHAL, VITRA, YAMAHA ETC. HE HAS WON SEVERAL COMPASSO D'ORO AWARDS AND MANY OTHER INTERNATIONAL ARCHITECTURAL AWARDS. 25 OF HIS DESIGNS ARE NOW IN THE PERMANENT COLLECTION OF THE MUSEUM OF MODERN ART IN NEW YORK, WHICH HONOURED HIM WITH A ONE-MAN SHOW IN 1987.

SINCE THE 1980s, HE HAS WORKED SUCCESSFULLY AS AN ARCHITECT IN EUROPE, UNITED ARAB EMIRATES, JAPAN, USA AND AUSTRALIA. HIS BEST KNOWN ACHIEVEMENTS INCLUDE:
IN **ITALY** - THE NEW FAIR DISTRICT OF THE *MILAN TRADE FAIR*, THE *EXHIBITION AND CONGRESS CENTRE* IN THE HISTORICAL PARK OF VILLA ERBA (CERNOBBIO, COMO), A BIG *CULTURAL CENTRE* IN TURIN (PROJECT NOW BEING IMPLEMENTED AFTER WINNING COMPETITION) AND THE *REDEVELOPMENT OF THE TRIESTE SEAFRONT* (INTERNATIONAL COMPETITION BY INVITATION, WINNING PROJECT FOR "HARBOUR TERMINAL")
IN **GERMANY** - THE NEW *ESSEN TRADES FAIR* AND A NEW *BUSINESS PARK* IN DÜSSELDORF (PROJECT NOW IMPLEMENTED AFTER WINNING COMPETITION).
IN **JAPAN** - *TOKYO DESIGN CENTER* AND *RISONARE VIVRE CLUB COMPLEX*, KOBUCHIZAWA.
IN **USA** - *NATUZZI AMERICAS HQ* (NORTH CAROLINA).
IN **AUSTRALIA** - THE EXTENSION TO THE *NATIONAL GALLERY OF VICTORIA* IN MELBOURNE (COMPETITION-WINNING, COMPLETED IN DECEMBER 2003).

AN AVID ART LOVER AND COLLECTOR, BELLINI IS ALSO WELL KNOWN AS AN ART EXHIBITION DESIGNER. MILESTONES IN THIS FIELD INCLUDE *"THE TREASURE OF ST MARK'S IN VENICE"* AT THE GRAND PALAIS IN PARIS AND OTHER MUSEUMS AROUND THE WORLD (1984-87), *"ITALIAN ART IN THE 20TH CENTURY"* AT THE ROYAL ACADEMY OF ARTS IN LONDON (1989), *"THE RENAISSANCE FROM BRUNELLESCHI TO MICHELANGELO"* AT PALAZZO GRASSI IN VENICE AND THEN IN PARIS AND BERLIN (1994-95), *"THE TRIUMPHS OF BAROQUE. ARCHITECTURE IN EUROPE 1600-1750"* AT THE STUPINIGI HUNTING LODGE IN TURIN (1999) AND *"CHRISTOPHER DRESSER. A DESIGNER AT THE COURT OF QUEEN VICTORIA"*, TRIENNALE, MILAN.

BELLINI HAS TAUGHT AND LECTURED AT NUMEROUS UNIVERSITIES AND INTERNATIONAL CULTURAL INSTITUTIONS. FROM 1986 TO 1991 HE WAS EDITOR OF DOMUS, THE PRESTIGIOUS ART, ARCHITECTURE AND DESIGN REVIEW. IN 1992 THE TOKYO DESIGN CENTER DEVOTED A MAJOR EXHIBITION TO HIS ARCHITECTURE AND DESIGN WORK, AND IN 1996 THE ROYAL INSTITUTE OF BRITISH ARCHITECTS (RIBA) HOSTED AN EXHIBITION OF HIS ARCHITECTURE. IN 2000 THE CIVIC CONTEMPORARY ART GALLEY IN TRENTO (ITALY) HOSTED THE ONE-MAN SHOW *"MARIO BELLINI: UN PERCORSO TRA ARCHITETTURE, MOBILI E MACCHINE"*, DESIGNED BY BELLINI HIMSELF. IN APRIL 2005, THE MILAN TRIENNALE WILL HOST A MONOGRAPHIC EXHIBITION ON HIS WORK.

DIRECTOR'S FOREWORD

IN PLANNING THE INAUGURAL EXHIBITIONS FOR THE RE-OPENING OF THE NATIONAL GALLERY OF VICTORIA, WE THOUGHT IT ONLY FITTING THAT ONE OF THE MAJOR EXHIBITIONS BE DEDICATED TO THE WORK OF THE ARCHITECT OF THE NGV REDEVELOPMENT, MARIO BELLINI. NOT ONLY IS BELLINI ONE OF THE PRE-EMINENT ARCHITECTS OF THE 20TH CENTURY, BUT HE IS ALSO ONE OF THE MOST VERSATILE AND INFLUENTIAL DESIGNERS OF HIS GENERATION. WE THEREFORE THOUGHT IT DOUBLY FITTING THAT *MARIO BELLINI: ARCHITECT AND DESIGNER* SHOULD INAUGURATE WHAT WILL BE AN ON-GOING PROGRAM OF EXHIBITIONS FOCUSSING ON THE BEST IN CONTEMPORARY ARCHITECTURE AND DESIGN.

BELLINI GRADUATED IN ARCHITECTURE FROM THE MILAN POLYTECHNIC IN 1959 AND FOR THE NEXT TWENTY YEARS FOCUSSED HIS ATTENTION ON FURNITURE AND INDUSTRIAL DESIGN, DEVELOPING HIS DISTINCTIVE AESTHETIC IN THE CONTEXT OF A DEEP RESPECT FOR THE MATERIALS AND CLASSICAL FORMS OF TRADITIONAL EUROPEAN AND ITALIAN CULTURE. THE VISUAL APPROACH TAKEN IN THIS EXHIBITION ALLOWS HIS SOURCES TO BE CLEARLY UNDERSTOOD. TO SAY THAT BELLINI IS A PROLIFIC DESIGNER IS AN UNDERSTATEMENT. FROM HIS ICONIC INDUSTRIAL DESIGNS FOR OLIVETTI TYPEWRITERS, LANDMARK FURNITURE FOR CASSINA, B&B ITALIA AND VITRA (ESPECIALLY THE CELEBRATED CAB SERIES), ELECTRONIC EQUIPMENT FOR BRIONVEGA AND YAMAHA AND LIGHTING FOR ARTEMIDE, FLOS AND ERCO, BELLINI'S NAME HAS BECOME SYNONYMOUS WITH A LEVEL OF EXCELLENCE ASSOCIATED WITH CONTEMPORARY ITALIAN DESIGN. SUCH IS BELLINI'S REPUTATION AS A DESIGNER THAT HE WAS ONE OF THE FIRST DESIGNERS TO BE ACCORDED A ONE-MAN SHOW DURING HIS LIFETIME AT THE MUSEUM OF MODERN ART IN NEW YORK.

ALTHOUGH BELLINI HAS ALWAYS RETAINED A COMMITMENT TO DESIGN WORK THROUGHOUT HIS CELEBRATED FORTY-YEAR CAREER, IT HAS TO BE SAID THAT OVER THE LAST TWENTY YEARS HE HAS CONCENTRATED ON A NUMBER OF MAJOR INTERNATIONAL ARCHITECTURAL PROJECTS RANGING FROM THE TOKYO DESIGN CENTRE, THE EXTENSION TO THE MILAN TRADE FAIR AND THE INTERNATIONAL CONGRESS AND EXHIBITION CENTRE IN CERNOBBIO. MOST RECENTLY, HE HAS WON THE COMPETITION FOR A LARGE AND SIGNIFICANT CULTURAL CENTRE COMBINING A PUBLIC LIBRARY AND THEATRE IN TURIN TO BE COMPLETED AT A COST OF 120 MILLION EUROS.

THE TOTAL REDEVELOPMENT OF THE NATIONAL GALLERY OF VICTORIA, A PROJECT SPANNING MORE THAN SEVEN YEARS AND COSTING A TOTAL OF 168 MILLION DOLLARS, IS THE LATEST COMPLETED PROJECT IN BELLINI'S DISTINGUISHED CAREER. IT IS TRUE TO SAY THAT BELLINI'S PRE-EMINENCE AS A DESIGNER IS PERFECTLY BALANCED BY HIS ARCHITECTURAL WORK AND MY COLLEAGUES AND I HAVE HAD THE GOOD FORTUNE TO WITNESS FIRST-HAND IN MANY MEETINGS, AND IN MANY WALKS AROUND OUR BUILDING SITE, THE SOPHISTICATION OF HIS EYE, AND HIS FAULTLESS SENSE OF FORM, LINE AND COLOUR. SOMETIMES THE SIMPLEST AND MOST SUBTLE OF VARIATIONS HAS TRANSFORMED THE VISUAL APPEARANCE OF KEY PARTS OF OUR BUILDING. BELLINI'S STYLE IS ELEGANT, MINIMALIST AND YET ALWAYS APPROPRIATE; CLASSIC IN THE MOST GENERAL SENSE.

BELLINI HAS ALSO HAD A DISTINGUISHED CAREER AS A DESIGNER OF ART EXHIBITIONS. THE MANY MEMORABLE EXHIBITIONS HE HAS DESIGNED INCLUDE *THE TREASURES OF VENICE* (GRAND PALAIS, PARIS, WHICH ALSO CAME TO THE NGV IN 1997), *ITALIAN ART IN THE 20TH CENTURY* (ROYAL ACADEMY, LONDON), *THE RENAISSANCE FROM BRUNELLESCHI TO MICHELANGELO: THE REPRESENTATION OF ARCHITECTURE* (PALAZZO GRASSI) AND MOST RECENTLY *THE TRIUMPHS OF THE BAROQUE: ARCHITECTURE IN EUROPE 1600-1750* (PALAZZO GRASSI). IT IS WORTH POINTING OUT THAT IN 1999, WE ENTERED INTO A SEPARATE CONTRACTUAL ARRANGEMENT WITH MARIO BELLINI TO WORK WITH OUR DESIGN DEPARTMENT ON THE EXHIBITION INSTALLATIONS. THE OPPORTUNITY TO INVOLVE THE HAND OF MARIO BELLINI IN THE PRESENTATION OF THE NGV WAS ONE NOT TO BE PASSED UP AND WE WERE DELIGHTED THAT BELLINI AND HIS TEAM ACCEPTED THE CHALLENGE WITH GUSTO. THE RESULT IS EVIDENT IN EVERY ASPECT OF THE BUILDING AND THE INSTALLATION OF THE COLLECTIONS. WHEREVER POSSIBLE, WE HAVE INCORPORATED BELLINI DESIGN IN OUR BUILDING, SUCH AS THE BELLINI CHAIRS IN OUR CAFÉ AND RESTAURANT. WE ARE PARTICULARLY PLEASED THAT BELLINI HAS DESIGNED EXCLUSIVELY FOR THE NGV A BENCH FOR THE GALLERY SPACES, AND A SERIES OF ELEGANT METAL PLINTHS FOR OUR SCULPTURES AND OTHER 3-D OBJECTS.

WE CAN THEREFORE REGARD THE REDEVELOPMENT OF THE NGV, ITS NEW ARCHITECTURE AND THE INSTALLATION OF THE COLLECTIONS AS AN EXAMPLE OF THE BEST IN CONTEMPORARY MILANESE DESIGN. IN DECEMBER 2003, MUSEUM VICTORIA WILL ALSO SHOWCASE ITALIAN DESIGN – INCLUDING THE WORK OF MARIO BELLINI – IN A COMPREHENSIVE EXHIBITION FROM THE TRIENNALE OF MILAN ENTITLED *DESIGN IN ITALY, 1945-2000.*

WHEN WE FIRST THOUGHT ABOUT THIS EXHIBITION, WE ANTICIPATED A FAIRLY TRADITIONAL PRESENTATION OF OBJECTS AND ARCHITECTURAL MODELS. IT WAS MARIO BELLINI HIMSELF WHO SUGGESTED THAT THE BEST WAY TO UNDERSTAND THE ESSENCE OF HIS STYLE WOULD BE VIA A DYNAMIC MULTI-MEDIA PRESENTATION, TRACING THE MANY AND VARIED AESTHETIC INFLUENCES ON BOTH HIS DESIGN AND ARCHITECTURAL CORPUS. THUS, I WOULD LIKE TO EXTEND MY WARMEST THANKS TO MARIO BELLINI, SENIOR ARCHITECTURAL ASSOCIATES, GIOVANNA BONFANTI AND GIOVANNI CAPPELLETTI, AND ALL AT MARIO BELLINI ASSOCIATI, MILAN, FOR THEIR ENTHUSIASTIC INVOLVEMENT IN THIS MOST FASCINATING OF PROJECTS. I WOULD ALSO LIKE TO ACKNOWLEDGE THE HARD WORK OF THE NGV CURATORIAL TEAM LED BY TONY ELLWOOD, DEPUTY DIRECTOR WITH TRACEY JUDD, CURATOR, INTERNATIONAL EXHIBITIONS, FOR THEIR DILIGENT MANAGEMENT OF THIS COMPLEX PROJECT. THANKS ALSO TO JEAN-PIERRE CHABROL, OUR MULTI-MEDIA DESIGNER, FOR PRODUCING SUCH AN EVOCATIVE DIGITAL PRESENTATION FOR THE EXHIBITION. FINALLY, I WOULD LIKE TO ACKNOWLEDGE THE SUPPORT OF BARRISOL FOR THEIR GENEROUS PROVISION OF THE ELEGANT FLOORING. MY WARM THANKS ALSO TO DIADEM AND DULUX FOR THEIR GENEROUS ASSISTANCE IN BRINGING THIS EXCITING PROJECT TO THE PUBLIC.

AS THE NGV HEADS INTO THE NEXT PHASE OF ITS 140-YEAR HISTORY, WE ARE ALL CONFIDENT THAT THE BUILDING, AS REDEVELOPED BY BELLINI, WILL WELCOME BACK OUR PAST DEDICATED AUDIENCES AS WELL AS A NEW GENERATION OF ART-LOVERS AND ARTISTS. FOR, IN BELLINI'S OWN WORDS: "GOOD ARCHITECTURE CAN HAVE A SERIES OF NEW LIVES".

GERARD VAUGHAN
DIRECTOR NGV

#01
NAMENATIONAL GALLERY OF VICTORIA
DESCRIPTIONEXHIBITION GALLERY
CLIENTNGV (AUSTRALIA)
YEARS1996 - 2003
LOCATIONMELBOURNE, AUSTRALIA
SURFACE33.000 SQ. M

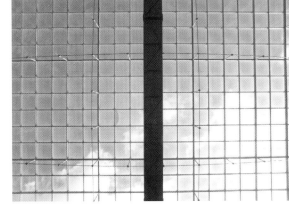

#02
NAME VILLA ERBA CONGRESS CENTRE
DESCRIPTION EXHIBITION AND CONFERENCE CENTRE
CLIENT VILLA ERBA SPA (ITALY)
YEARS 1986 - 1990
LOCATION CERNOBBIO, COMO, ITALY
SURFACE 14.000 SQ. M

#03
NAMEPORTELLO MILAN TRADE FAIR
DESCRIPTIONNEW DISTRICT OF MILAN TRADE FAIR
CLIENTENTE AUTONOMO FIERA DI MILANO (ITALY)
YEARS1987 - 1997
LOCATIONPORTELLO AREA, MILAN, ITALY
SURFACE106.000 SQ. M

#04
NAME**TOKYO DESIGN CENTER**
DESCRIPTION**MULTI-STOREY BUILDING FOR FURNITURE SHOWROOM**
CLIENT**SOWA SHOJI CO. (JAPAN)**
YEARS**1988 - 1992**
LOCATION**HIGASHI GOTANDA, TOKYO, JAPAN**
SURFACE**12.000 SQ. M**

#05
NAMERISONARE VIVRE CLUB
DESCRIPTION200-ROOM COMPLEX WITH RESTAURANT, CONFERENCE
HALLS, AUDITORIUM, DISCO AND SPORT FACILITIES.
CLIENTVIVRE, NICHII CO. LTD (JAPAN)
YEARS1989 - 1992
LOCATIONKOBUCHIZAWA, YAMANASHI-KEN, JAPAN
SURFACE38.000 SQ. M

#06

NAME NATUZZI AMERICAS - HEADQUARTERS
DESCRIPTION MULTI-STOREY BUILDING FOR
FURNITURE SHOWROOM AND OFFICES,
WITH AN OPEN-AIR SHOWROOM TERRACE.
CLIENT NATUZZI AMERICAS INC (USA)
YEARS 1996 - 1998
LOCATION HIGH POINT, NORTH CAROLINA, USA
SURFACE 10.000 SQ. M

#07
NAMEARSOA - HEADQUARTERS
DESCRIPTIONNEW HEADQUARTERS OF ARSOA COSMETIC CO.
(OFFICES, RESEARCH & DEVELOPMENT DEPT.)
CLIENTARSOA OSHO CO. LTD (JAPAN)
YEARS1996 - 1998
LOCATIONKOBUCHIZAWA, YAMANASHI-KEN, JAPAN
SURFACE9.000 SQ. M

#08
NAMETURIN CULTURAL CENTRE
DESCRIPTIONCULTURAL COMPLEX INCLUDING PUBLIC LIBRARY AND THEATRE.
INTERNATIONAL COMPETITION WINNER.
PROJECT NOW BEING IMPLEMENTED.
CLIENTCITY OF TURIN (ITALY)
YEARS2001 - IN PROGRESS
LOCATIONTURIN, ITALY
SURFACE40.000 SQ. M

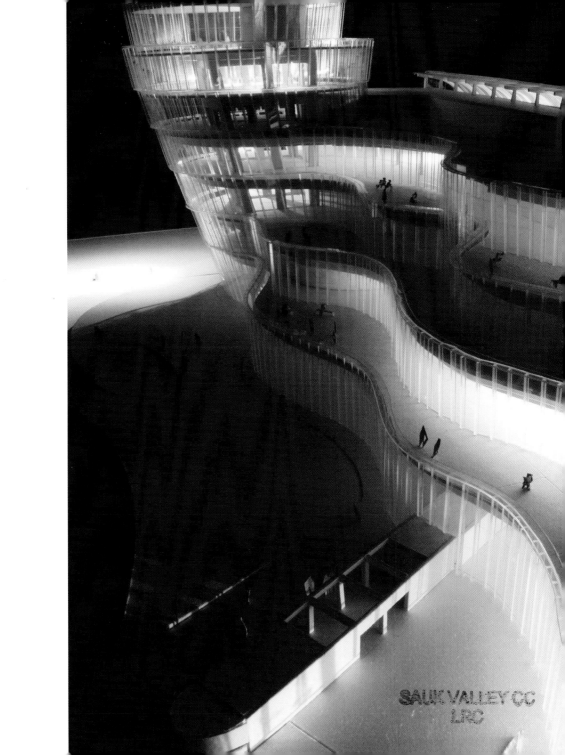

SAUK VALLEY CC
LRC

NAME GOSHIKIDAI MARINE RESORT
DESCRIPTION COMPLEX COMPRISING RESIDENCES,
SHOPPING CENTER, CULTURAL AND ENTERTAINMENT
AMENITIES AND A TOURIST PORT.
CLIENT NIISHI CO., LTD. OSAKA (JAPAN)
YEARS 1992 - 1993
LOCATION GOSHIKIDAI, KAGAWA-KEN, JAPAN
SURFACE 65.000 SQ. M

#10
NAME MAB. ZEIL PROJECT
DESCRIPTION INTERNATIONAL COMPETITION BY INVITATION.
BELLINI IS AMONG THE THREE WINNING GROUPS.
CLIENT MAB PROJEKTENTWICKLUNG GMBH (GERMANY)
YEAR 2002
LOCATION FRANKFURT AM MAIN (GERMANY)
SURFACE 115.000 SQ. M

#11
NAMENEW CAMPUS FOR MILAN POLYTECHNIC
DESCRIPTIONCOMPETITION BY INVITATION.
PROJECT RECEIVED A SPECIAL MENTION.
CLIENTMILAN TOWN COUNCIL AND
AZIENDA ELLETRICA MUNICIPALE (AEM) SPA (ITALY)
YEAR1998
LOCATIONMILAN, ITALY
SURFACE427.500 SQ. M

#12

NAMEHAIHE WATERFRONT
DESCRIPTIONINTERNATIONAL LIMITED
COMPETITION. BELLINI IS AMONG THE THREE
GROUPS SELECTED FOR THE FIRST PHASE.
CLIENTTIAN JIN TOWN COUNCIL (CHINA)
YEAR2003
LOCATIONTIAN JIN, CHINA
SURFACE300.000 SQ. M

#13
NAME YOKOHAMA BUSINESS PARK
DESCRIPTION MASTER PLAN, PLAZA AND CONCOURSE.
PUBLIC SPACES AND FACILITIES FOR THE BUSINESS PARK.
CLIENT NOMURA REAL ESTATE DEV., TOKYO (JAPAN)
YEARS 1987 - 1991
LOCATION YOKOHAMA, JAPAN
SURFACE 71.000 SQ. M

#14
NAMEOFFICES AND INDUSTRIAL COMPLEX
DESCRIPTIONSPACES FOR SERVICE ACTIVITIES AND INDUSTRIAL USE.
CLIENTSCOTTI IMMOBILIARE SPA, MILANO (ITALY)
YEARS1984 - 1988
LOCATIONMILAN, ITALY
SURFACE31.000 SQ. M

#15
NAME CASSINA JAPAN SHOWROOM
DESCRIPTION CASSINA SHOWROOM
CLIENT CASSINA JAPAN INC. (JAPAN)
YEAR 1989
LOCATION MINAMI AOYAMA COLLEZIONE BULDING,
TOKYO, JAPAN
SURFACE 300 SQ. M

#16
NAMETHE RENAISSANCE FROM
BRUNELLESCHI TO MICHELANGELO.
THE REPRESENTATION OF ARCHITECTURE
DESCRIPTIONEXHIBITION DESIGN
CLIENTPALAZZO GRASSI (ITALY)
YEARS1994 - 1995
LOCATIONSPALAZZO GRASSI,VENICE/MUSÈE
NATIONAL DES MONUMENTS FRANÇAIS,PARIS/
ALTES MUSEUM, BERLIN
SURFACE1.600 SQ. M

NAMERISONARE VIVRE CLUB
DESCRIPTION200-ROOM COMPLEX WITH
RESTAURANT, CONFERENCE HALLS,
AUDITORIUM, DISCO AND SPORT FACILITIES.
CLIENTVIVRE, NICHII CO. LTD (JAPAN)
YEARS1989-1992
LOCATIONKOBUCHIZAWA, YAMANASHI-KEN, JAPAN
SURFACE38.000 SQ. M

NAMETRADE FAIR EXTENSION, ESSEN
DESCRIPTIONEXTENSION TO ESSEN INTERNATIONAL
TRADE FAIR AND REDESIGN OF GRUGA PARK.
INTERNATIONAL COMPETITION WINNER.
CLIENTMESSE ESSEN GMBH (GERMANY)
YEARS1997-2001
LOCATIONESSEN, GERMANY
SURFACE104.000 SQ. M

Harmony Space

Leather Space

Harmony Spa

#19
NAME NATUZZI COLOGNE
DESCRIPTION TRADE FARE SHOWROOM
CLIENT NATUZZI (ITALY)
YEAR 2002
LOCATION COLOGNE, GERMANY
SURFACE 1.700 SQ. M

#20
NAME THE TRIUMPHS OF THE BAROQUE.
ARCHITECTURE IN EUROPE, 1600 - 1750
DESCRIPTION EXHIBITION DESIGN
CLIENT PALAZZO GRASSI, VENICE (ITALY)
YEARS 1998 - 1999
LOCATION TURIN, ITALY
SURFACE 3.000 SQ. M

#21
NAME ROSENTHAL SHOWROOM
DESCRIPTION FAIR SHOWROOM
CLIENT ROSENTHAL AG (GERMANY)
YEAR 1992
LOCATION COLOGNE, GERMANY
SURFACE 600 SQ. M

#22
NAME CHRISTOPHER DRESSER. A DESIGNER AT THE COURT OF QUEEN VICTORIA
DESCRIPTION EXHIBITION DESIGN
CLIENT TRIENNALE DI MILANO (ITALY)
YEAR 2001 - 2002
LOCATION TRIENNALE, MILAN, ITALY
SURFACE 1.000 SQ. M

ARTE
ISLAMICA

ARTE
BIZANTINA

#23
NAMETHE TREASURES OF ST. MARCO IN VENICE
DESCRIPTIONEXHIBITION DESIGN
CLIENTOLIVETTI SPA (ITALY)
YEARS1984 - 1987
LOCATIONSPARIS, FRANCE
COLOGNE, GERMANY
LONDON, UK
NEW YORK, USA
LOS ANGELES, USA
DALLAS, USA
CHICAGO, USA
ROME, ITALY
MILAN, ITALY
VENICE, ITALY

NAMENATUZZI AMERICAS - HEADQUARTERS
DESCRIPTIONMULTI-STOREY BUILDING FOR
FURNITURE SHOWROOM AND OFFICES,
WITH AN OPEN-AIR SHOWROOM TERRACE.
CLIENTNATUZZI AMERICAS INC. (USA)
YEARS1996 - 1998
LOCATIONHIGH POINT, NORTH CAROLINA, USA
SURFACE10.000 SQ. M

#25
NAMEMARIO BELLINI DESIGNER
DESCRIPTIONEXHIBITION DESIGN
CLIENTMoMA NEW YORK (USA)
YEAR1987
LOCATIONMoMA, NEW YORK, USA
SURFACE400 SQ. M

#26
NAME ITALIAN ART IN THE 20TH CENTURY
DESCRIPTION EXHIBITION DESIGN
CLIENT ROYAL ACADEMY OF ART, LONDON (UK)
YEAR 1989
LOCATION ROYAL ACADEMY OF ART, LONDON (UK)
SURFACE 1.000 SQ. M

#28
NAMECAB 413
DESCRIPTIONLEATHER UPHOLSTERED ARMCHAIR
CLIENTCASSINA SPA (ITALY)
YEAR1979

#31
NAME BELLINI CHAIR
DESCRIPTION POLYPROPYLENE STACKING CHAIR
CLIENT HELLER INC. (USA)
YEAR 1998

#32
NAME FAUST
DESCRIPTION SOFA COLLECTION
CLIENT DRIADE SPA (ITALY)
YEAR 2001

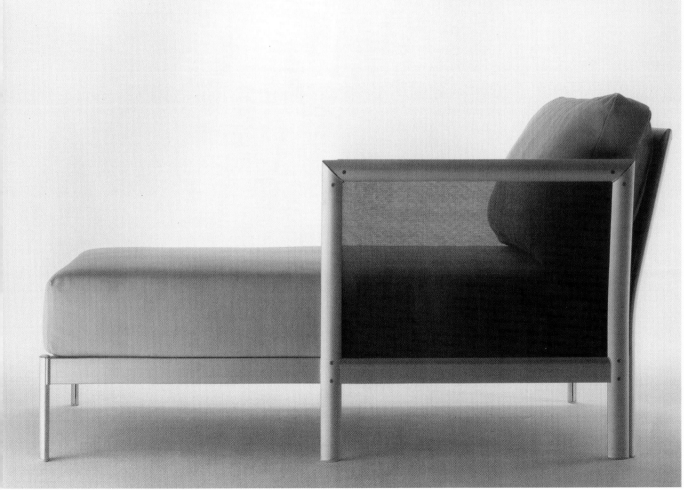

#34
NAME ETP 55
DESCRIPTION PORTABLE ELECTRONIC TYPEWRITER
CLIENT OLIVETTI SPA (ITALY)
YEAR 1987

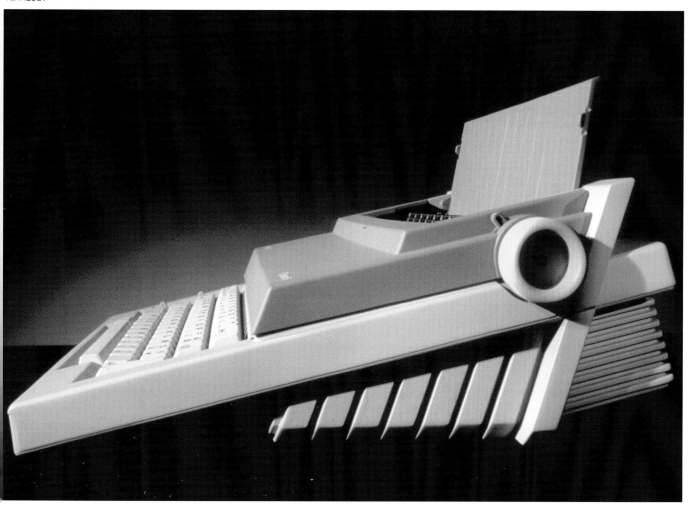

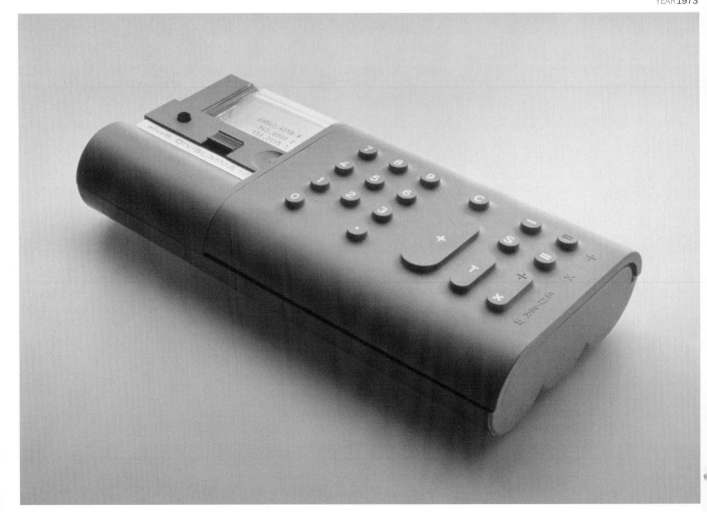

#36
NAMELE BAMBOLE
DESCRIPTIONDOMESTIC LOUNGE SEATING COLLECTION
CLIENTB&B SPA (ITALY)
YEAR1972

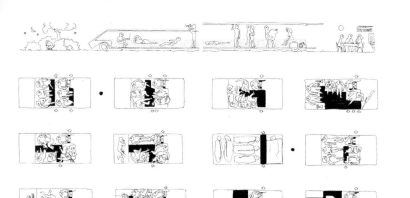

#37
NAME KAR-A-SUTRA
DESCRIPTION MOBILE LIVING CONCEPT CAR
CLIENT MoMA NEW YORK (USA)
YEAR 1972

#38
NAME POP
DESCRIPTION PORTABLE RECORD PLAYER
CLIENT MINERVA SPA (ITALY)
YEAR 1968

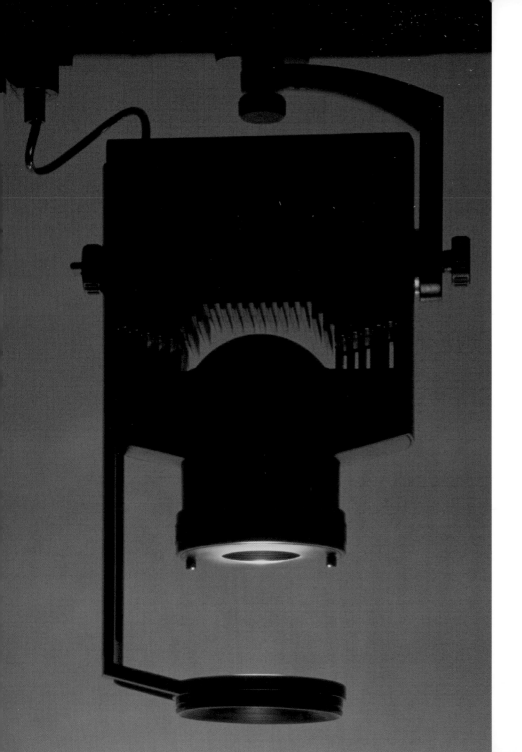

#39
NAMEECLIPSE
DESCRIPTIONSPOT LIGHTING SYSTEM
CLIENTERCO LEUCHTEN GMBH (GERMANY)
YEAR1986

#40
NAME TOTEM
DESCRIPTION SOUND SYSTEM WITH
DETACHABLE SPEAKERS
CLIENT BRIONVEGA SPA (ITALY)
YEAR 1971

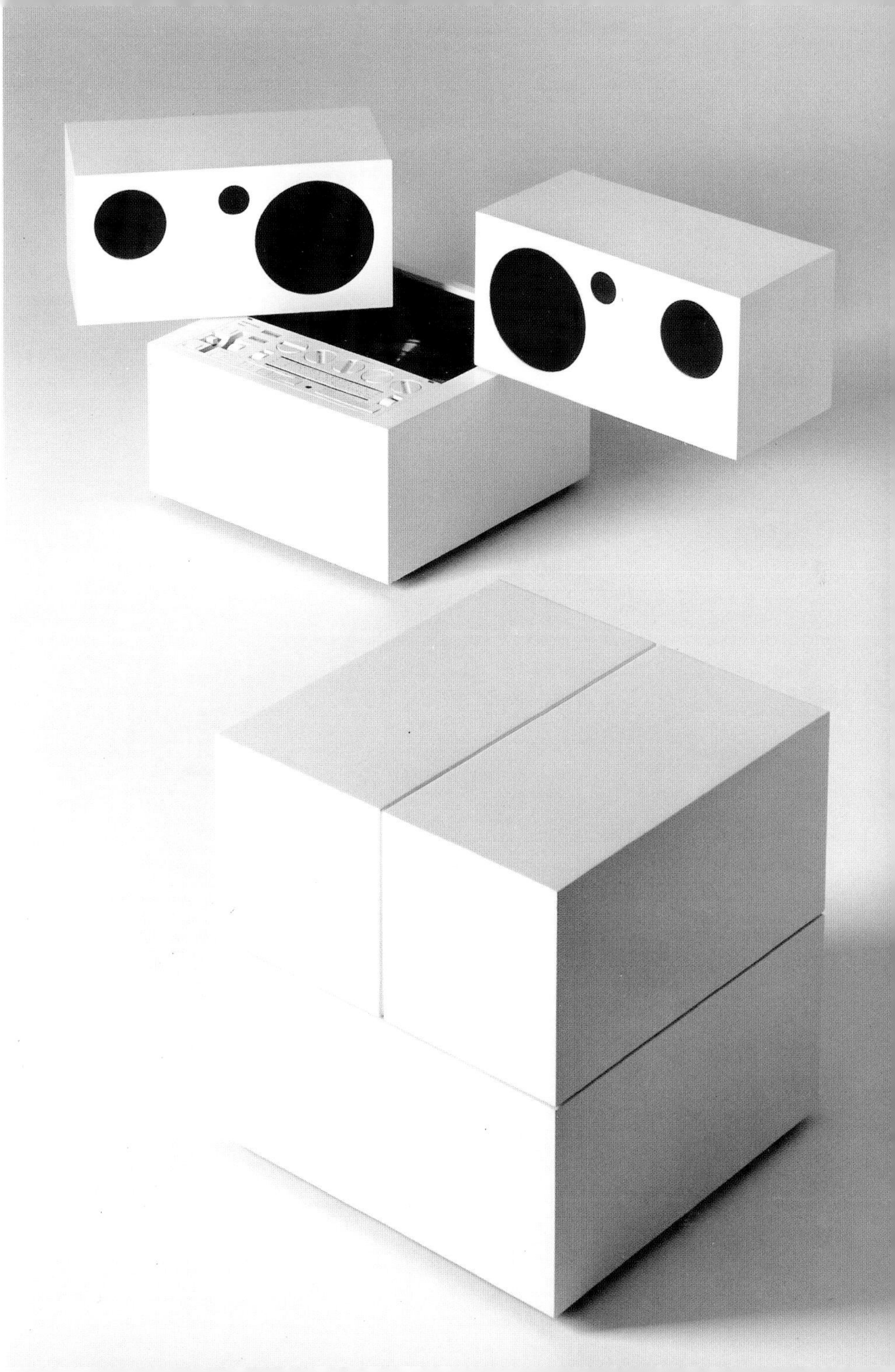

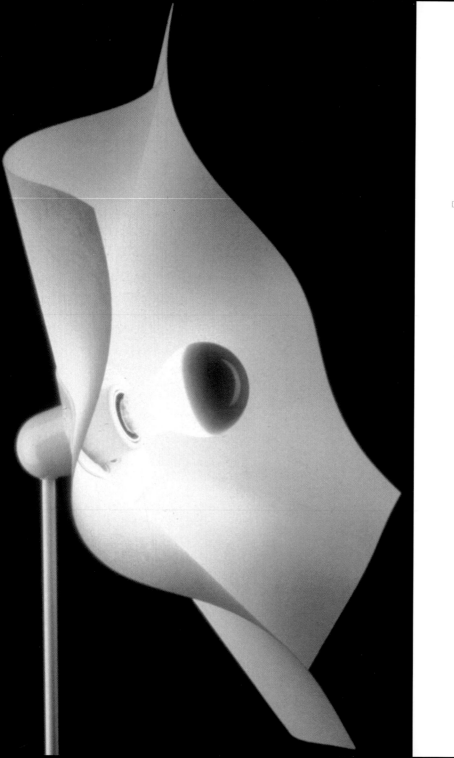

#41
NAMEAREA
DESCRIPTIONDOMESTIC LIGHTING RANGE
CLIENTARTEMIDE SPA (ITALY)
YEAR1974

#42
NAME PERSONA
DESCRIPTION OFFICE CHAIR
CLIENT VITRA INTERNATIONAL AG (GERMANY)
YEAR 1984

NAMECLASS
DESCRIPTIONBATHROOM TAPS RANGE
CLIENTIDEAL STANDARD SPA (BELGIUM)
YEAR1987

#45
NAMEGIOIELLI
DESCRIPTIONJEWELLERY COLLECTION
CLIENTFARAONE (ITALY)
YEAR1979

#46
NAME SOGNI INFRANTI
DESCRIPTION VASE COLLECTION
CLIENT VENINI SPA (ITALY)
YEAR 1996

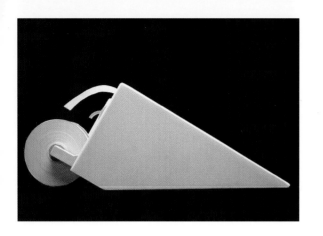

#47
NAME LOGOS 50/60
DESCRIPTION ELECTRONIC CALCULATOR
CLIENT OLIVETTI SPA (ITALY)
YEAR 1972

#48
NAME METROPOL
DESCRIPTION OFFICE FURNITURE SYSTEM
CLIENT VITRA INTERNATIONAL AG (GERMANY)
YEAR 1989

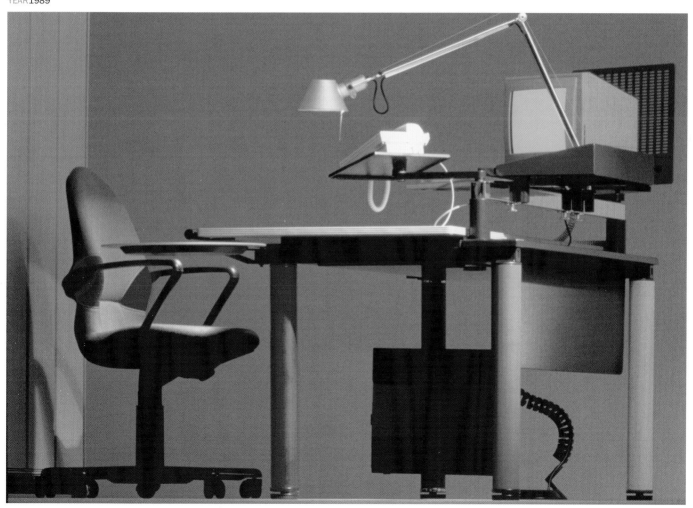

#49
NAME AMANTA
DESCRIPTION SOFA
CLIENT B&B SPA (ITALY)
YEAR 1966

#51
NAMEVOL AU VENT
DESCRIPTIONFULLY UPHOLSTERED CHAIR
CLIENTB&B SPA (ITALY)
YEAR2001

MARIO BELLINI

PUBLISHED BY THE NATIONAL GALLERY OF VICTORIA
180 ST. KILDA ROAD, MELBOURNE 3004

NATIONAL LIBRARY OF AUSTRALIA CATALOGUING-IN-PUBLICATION DATA

MARIO BELLINI: ARCHITECT AND DESIGNER

ISBN 0 7241 0240 X

1. BELLINI, MARIO, 1935- .
2. NATIONAL GALLERY OF VICTORIA.
3. ART MUSEUMS – VICTORIA – MELBOURNE.
4. ARCHITECTURE, MODERN. I. VAUGHAN, GERARD. II. NATIONAL GALLERY OF VICTORIA.

720.92

GRAPHIC DESIGN: ALEXANDER ÅHNEBRINK
PRINTED BY: TIPOLITOMAGGIONI, MILAN, ITALY